The Addison Wesley Longman Interactive Guide to *Newsweek*

A Hands-On Supplement for *Newsweek* Magazine

Shirley Russak Wachtel
Middlesex County College

Addison Wesley Longman

An imprint of Addison Wesley Longman, Inc.

New York • Reading, Massachusetts • Menlo Park, California • Harlow, England
Don Mills, Ontario • Sydney • Mexico City • Madrid • Amsterdam

Acquisitions Editor: Steven Rigolosi
Supplements Editor: Donna Campion
Text Design: Digital Text Construction
Electronic Page Makeup: Digital Text Construction

The Addison Wesley Longman Interactive Guide to *Newsweek* by Shirley Russak Wachtel

ISBN 0-321-05528-4

02—VG—98765

Table of Contents

Introduction to Instructors

Ask any student who doesn't like to read the reason why, and most will answer that they're simply not interested in the material. That's why *Newsweek* is perfectly suited to the needs of the classroom. By providing an array of spirited and relevant feature articles, essays, and reviews on subjects from politics to entertainment, *Newsweek* captures and holds the interest of even the most stubborn non-reader. And now, for the first time, an interactive guide to *Newsweek* is available for the classroom.

For the teacher, the *Interactive Guide to Newsweek* contains an assortment of timely articles, book and movie reviews, and powerful graphics, all of which have made *Newsweek* a frontrunner in the consumer information market. This relevant and interesting subject matter provides the motivation students need to build their reading skills. The readings may be used alone or in conjunction with articles found in *Newsweek* each week. This Interactive Guide offers worksheets with generic questions that can be applied to any *Newsweek* material chosen. These worksheets (perforated for facility) focus on development of literal and critical comprehension skills, and offer assignments for extended writing. Suggestions for research, collaborative activities, and various forms of interactive work are also included.

For the student, the *Interactive Guide to Newsweek* acts not only as a stimulating introduction to current affairs, but helps to foster the reading skills so necessary as one proceeds through college courses and the profession of choice. The questions included with each worksheet make it easy to understand the vocabulary and main idea, while helping students draw conclusions about each of the readings. Furthermore, the worksheets encourage the reader to discuss and write about the articles, reviews, photos, and cartoons that appear in *Newsweek*.

Whether your interest lies in money, science, music, or sports, there is something in *Newsweek* for you. So, welcome to *Newsweek* and the *Interactive Guide to Newsweek*—enjoy it, challenge yourself, and above all, read!

Unit 1

Newsweek: An Overview

Newsweek at a Glance

Each week, you will find a series of features in *Newsweek*. These features are set off by headings that signal the type of material in the features. Here are the headings to look for:

Special Reports highlight a significant, often controversial, event in news feature format. Providing answers to the frequently asked journalist's questions, (*who, what, why, when, and where*), the special reports provide a comprehensive overview of timely issues. Opening with a quote, anecdote, or intriguing scene, the ***introduction*** stimulates interest in the topic. The ***body*** develops the article's premise with a detailed account or an analysis of the topic or event. Peppered with quotes, photographs, charts, and other graphics, the report offers a thorough and thought-provoking picture of the issue. The ***conclusion*** sums up the major points, with final comments that often stimulate thought. ***Sidebars*** (smaller accompanying articles) round out the coverage.

International News offers the same feature articles as Special Reports, with a focus on events across the world.

National Affairs offer the same type of balanced, intriguing coverage as Special Reports, with an eye toward national events.

Society includes articles covering a variety of topics on social institutions including health, religion, education, and the media.

Lifestyle provides a review of features that reflect current trends in areas such as architecture, psychology, sports, and publishing.

The Arts covers issues in art, music, shows, movies, and literature.

Focus on Money often appears to highlight issues like the stock market, retirement, and home-buying.

Departments include the following regular reports, each no more than a page or two, with subjects often presented in single paragraph format:

- *Periscope* offers bits of information on political or cultural affairs. Its "Conventional Wisdom Watch" provides a playful look at the current "ups and downs" of figures in the public eye.
- *Cyberscope* provides the latest news of the computer scene.
- *Millennium* offers a page-long assessment of what we can look forward to as we enter the new century.
- *My Turn* consists of a persuasive essay expressing a reader's opinion on a controversial topic.
- *Letters* is a compendium of readers' responses to previous articles in the magazine.
- *Perspectives* is an amusing and incisive series of quotes by personalities on the current scene, along with editorial cartoons that provoke a closer look at the issues.
- *Newsmakers* puts leading figures in entertainment and the media under the microscope's lens, adding insight to their comings and goings.
- *The Last Word* is aptly named, for here on the magazine's last page, the reader finds

essays by respected columnists like Meg Greenfield and Robert Samuelson, presenting a perspective on current issues.

Advertisements, which are the mainstay of any publication, are often overlooked as educational material. They abound in *Newsweek* and offer the opportunity for analysis of advertising techniques and consumer habits.

Using *Newsweek* to Improve Reading Skills

Being a successful reader means being an *active* reader. Your subscription to *Newsweek* and this Interactive Guide can help you improve the three major areas of reading comprehension: ***literal***, ***critical***, and ***affective***.

Literal Comprehension

Literal Comprehension involves an understanding of the written word at its most basic level. The skills associated with literal comprehension include 1) vocabulary, 2) main idea, 3) rhetorical modes, and 4) study techniques. The worksheets in this book are designed to reinforce comprehension in each of these skills.

Vocabulary: Vocabulary knowledge constitutes the building blocks of reading comprehension. Understanding the meaning of words is most often attained through the ***context***. (That's why people who read a lot often know an abundance of words!) This workbook offers you the opportunity to use newly-acquired words in sentences of your own and to incorporate these new words into your own vocabulary.

You may also learn through an understanding of ***word parts*** (prefix, suffix, root), and by looking up the meaning in a ***dictionary***. Your textbook will offer lists of these word parts. In this workbook,"One More Word" features ask you to find another word (not included in the list distributed by your instructor), define it, and explain how you were able to determine its meaning.

Main Idea: Finding the main idea of a reading selection is probably the most essential reading skill you need to know. If you can understand the main idea (also known as *main point, controlling* idea, *central thesis*, or *gist*), you will be able to grasp the meaning of the material. The main idea should not be confused with the ***topic***, which is the general subject and is often represented in a title or headline.

The ***main idea***, or ***topic sentence***, of a reading selection always 1) is a complete sentence, 2) conveys a message 3) has a point of view (a way of looking at something). The topic sentence may be found anywhere in a paragraph, or it may even be implied. The main idea of an entire article or essay is called the ***thesis.***

The ***major details*** support the main idea directly, while ***minor details*** (indirect support sometimes in the form of quotes or responses) indirectly support the main idea. Students are sometimes confused by what they read because many complicated details may cloud the meaning. However, once you are able to locate the main idea, you can attain a basic understanding of anything you read.

Together, the topic, main idea, and details form an article or essay. Each work has an ***introduction***, which introduces the reader in a clear, sometimes imaginative way, to the material. The

body contains the details that support the thesis or main idea. Finally, the ***conclusion*** summarizes the major points, often leaving the reader with "food for thought."

This Interactive Guide to *Newsweek* recognizes the importance of main idea, so all worksheets include a question that asks you to identify the main idea and state it in your own words. You will also be asked to state the topic and list the details that support the main idea. In addition, you will be asked to identify the reporter's Five W's: *who, what, why* , *when*, and *where.* Answering these questions will help you find and understand the main idea.

Rhetorical Modes: ***Rhetorical modes*** are patterns in which an article's details are organized. These patterns include

- illustration or example
- definition
- comparison/contrast
- sequence of events
- cause and effect
- description
- narration

You can find more details on these patterns of organization in your textbook. In the worksheets included here, you will be asked to examine various articles and essays, and identify the patterns of organization.

Study Techniques: A popular method of study is the ***SQ3R*** approach, which can be applied to *Newsweek* articles and just about any college discipline.

- "S" stands for **survey.** To get a general sense of the articles preread the headline, subheadings, words written in boldface or italics, and the introductions and conclusions.
- "Q" is for **question.** To maintain interest in the reading, turn a statement into a question. For example, the statement "An important scientific discovery was made last week," might be converted to "What was the important scientific discovery made last week?" The process makes sense; once you pose a question, you will read on to attain the answer.
- "R" means **read**. After you have surveyed and questioned, you can now read the article word for word, focusing on words in groups to get meaning from the context.
- The second "R", **recite**, is an important but often overlooked aspect of the study process. Until this stage, you have been absorbing the material. But recitation, or practice, is needed if you are to "give back" that material in the form of a research paper, discussion, or exam. This step may take the form of oral recitation, annotation, taking notes, or creating more formal outlines, maps, or summaries.
- The third "R" means **review.** In this stage, you skim through the selection and answer questions immediately after the reading and prior to an exam.

The Interactive Guide to *Newsweek* aids you through the SQ3R procedure by posing questions that reinforce proper study habits. Try the SQ3R method—it really works!

Critical Comprehension

Once you have achieved a literal comprehension of a reading selection,you are ready for the next step, gaining an understanding on a critical level. ***Critical comprehension*** is simply the ability to interpret what is read. Skills incorporated in critical reading include: 1) distinguishing fact from opinion; 2) recognizing writer's intent, attitude, and tone; 3) recognizing inference and drawing conclusions; and 4) understanding bias.

Fact versus opinion: A ***fact*** is anything that can be proven. For example, a statement such as "this room measures 20 by 30 feet" may be proven true simply by measuring the room. If the room measurement does not agree with the statement, then the statement is incorrect. An ***opinion*** is a statement that can be disputed. For example, the sentence "This is a comfortable room" would be considered an opinion because the statement is an observation that can be disputed.

Readers of *Newsweek* often see both fact and opinion in feature articles, which present both factual evidence and opinionated quotes. Questions in this workbook ask you to identify both facts and opinions in *Newsweek* articles and in persuasive essays such as "My Turn" and "The Last Word." You will also be asked to differentiate the rhetorical modes that support the opinions presented. For example, ***argument*** based on reason is used to prove a concept true or false. ***Persuasion*** uses facts to convince the reader to change his or her opinion and behavior. Effective editorials or columns usually employ both of these rhetorical modes.

Intent, attitude, and tone: A well-crafted persuasive essay or news story uses intent, attitude, and tone to add shades of meaning to the piece.

- The writer's ***intent*** is simply his or her purpose for writing the article. For example, the intent may be to educate, entertain, or argue a point. An understanding of intent is important because it determines how the writer approaches the material.
- The writer's ***attitude*** shows how he or she feels about the subject.
- The writer's ***tone*** is reflected in how the writer expresses himself or herself, and often is what makes a piece memorable.
- ***Irony*** is a popular device used in expressing tone; it is an outcome which is contrary, or opposite, to what is expected. For example, it is ironic when someone who always remembers an umbrella forgets it on the one day it rains.
- ***Figurative language*** is often used to compare two different things. A ***simile*** compares things using the words "like" or "as," as in "He was as tall as a tree." A ***metaphor*** compares things without using "like" or "as," as in "She is an angel." ***Personification*** gives a nonhuman object human characteristics, as in "The thirsty flowers stretched toward the sun." ***Hyperbole*** is an exaggeration using comparison to emphasize a point, as in "She was as hungry as a bear."

Throughout this Interactive Guide to *Newsweek*, you will learn to identify a writer's intent, attitude, and tone as you analyze various articles and respond to questions in the Worksheets.

Recognizing inference and drawing conclusions: *Inference* is meaning that is received indirectly, or hinted at in the text. Using literal reading skills and then applying critical skills, readers are able to infer a deeper meaning from the language. For example, if a writer describes a house that is ornate and has servant's quarters, a tennis court on premises, and a magnificent swimming pool, the writer may then infer that the person living there is rich. The adept reader also draws ***conclusions*** from essays that present facts and opinions. Reading and answering questions regarding the "My Turn" and "The Last Word" essays in *Newsweek* are perfect ways to practice these critical skills.

Bias: ***Bias*** is a prejudice, or a slanted view of something. Writings that exhibit bias are said to be ***subjective***. Those that do not reveal bias are ***objective.*** The astute reader learns how to recognize bias while evaluating an article, and then comes to his or her own conclusions. Sometimes, the presence of bias is quite clear, as in ***editorials,*** which are by definition slanted toward one particular opinion. In other instances, bias can be found in unlikely sources, such as history textbooks that present only one side of an event or omit the accomplishments of a particular group. While such bias may not be intended, it is important that the reader realize that a complete, balanced picture is not being presented. *Newsweek* contains several articles in which people with certain biases are quoted. Persuasive essays and, of course, ads in the magazine contain bias that is intentional.

Affective Comprehension

Affective reading is the highest order of comprehension, and can be attained only with both a literal and a critical understanding of the material. Simply stated, ***affective comprehension*** reflects how the reader is "affected" by articles, essays, pictures, or even ads. It is an emotional or intellectually charged reaction to the work. Whenever anyone cries, laughs, or becomes angry or frightened by a reading, then affective comprehension is attained. Everyone wants to be moved or stimulated by material, and that is exactly why people enjoy reading! Readers of *Newsweek* learn to grasp its pages on both literal and critical levels; questions presented in the *Interactive Guide to Newsweek* are designed to measure affective reactions.

Now . . . on to some selections from *Newsweek.* Enjoy your subscription!

Unit 2

Understanding the News

Cover Stories
Special Reports,
International News,
and Current Affairs

Newsweek Worksheet

The Cover Story

Name____________________

Class __________ **Date**__________

The adage "A picture is worth a thousand words" is often true. Evocative snapshots or powerful graphics have emotional appeal, enhance the meaning of an article, and spark interest. This is especially true of cover stories and images, which are designed to capture attention and increase readership.

Take a look at the cover page of the current issue of *Newsweek.*

Why do you think this photograph was chosen to accompany this article?

Is the cover photo candid, posed or created by computer? Is this image well-chosen to help explain the article's meaning? Explain.

Now, read the cover story. Do you think the cover photo was effective? Why or why not? Would you have chosen another picture for the front page? Why or why not?

Newsweek Worksheet

The Cover Story

Name______________________________

Class ______________ **Date**______________

The adage "A picture is worth a thousand words" is often true. Evocative snapshots or powerful graphics have emotional appeal, enhance the meaning of an article, and spark interest. This is especially true of cover stories and images, which are designed to capture attention and increase readership.

Take a look at the cover page of the current issue of *Newsweek.*

Why do you think this photograph was chosen to accompany this article?

Is the cover photo candid, posed or created by computer? Is this image well-chosen to help explain the article's meaning? Explain.

Now, read the cover story. Do you think the cover photo was effective? Why or why not? Would you have chosen another picture for the front page? Why or why not?

Newsweek Worksheet

The Cover Story

Name______________________________

Class _______________ **Date**_______________

The adage "A picture is worth a thousand words" is often true. Evocative snapshots or powerful graphics have emotional appeal, enhance the meaning of an article, and spark interest. This is especially true of cover stories and images, which are designed to capture attention and increase readership.

Take a look at the cover page of the current issue of *Newsweek.*

Why do you think this photograph was chosen to accompany this article?

____

____

____

____

Is the cover photo candid, posed or created by computer? Is this image well-chosen to help explain the article's meaning? Explain.

____

____

Now, read the cover story. Do you think the cover photo was effective? Why or why not? Would you have chosen another picture for the front page? Why or why not?

____

____

____

____

____

____

____

____

____

Newsweek Worksheet

The Cover Story

Name ______________________________

Class ________________ **Date** ________________

The adage "A picture is worth a thousand words" is often true. Evocative snapshots or powerful graphics have emotional appeal, enhance the meaning of an article, and spark interest. This is especially true of cover stories and images, which are designed to capture attention and increase readership.

Take a look at the cover page of the current issue of *Newsweek.*

Why do you think this photograph was chosen to accompany this article?

____

____

____

____

Is the cover photo candid, posed or created by computer? Is this image well-chosen to help explain the article's meaning? Explain.

____

____

Now, read the cover story. Do you think the cover photo was effective? Why or why not? Would you have chosen another picture for the front page? Why or why not?

____

____

____

____

____

____

____

____

____

Newsweek Worksheet

Understanding the News

Name ______________________

Class ______________ **Date** ______________

Choose a news article from the current issue of *Newsweek.* (Look for the heading "Special Report," "International News," or "National Affairs." Then complete this worksheet).

Ready **Survey** the material. Here's what I know about the subject:

____

Set **Question** yourself. Here's one thing I would like to know:

____

Go **Read.** (Remember to read words in groups without hesitating.)
Recite. (Annotate. Take notes in the margins.)
Review. Here's one thing I learned:

____

I. LITERAL COMPREHENSION

Reporter's Questions

Who? ______________________

What? ______________________

Why? ______________________

When? ______________________

Where? ______________________

Topic ______________________

Main Idea ______________________

Three Details

1. ______________________
2. ______________________
3. ______________________

New Words (Plus definitions)

1. ______________________________

2. ______________________________

3. ______________________________

4. ______________________________

One more word! ______________________________

How I found it (context, word parts, dictionary) ______________________________

How I use it ______________________________

II. CRITICAL COMPREHENSION

List two opinions (use quotes!)

1. ______________________________

2. ______________________________

The viewpoint of the article is ______________________________

III. AFFECTIVE COMPREHENSION

After reading this article, I believe ______________________________

____

____

____

____

QUESTIONS????

Newsweek Worksheet

Understanding the News

Name______________________________

Class ______________ **Date**______________

Choose a news article from the current issue of *Newsweek.* (Look for the heading "Special Report," "International News," or "National Affairs." Then complete this worksheet).

Ready **Survey** the material. Here's what I know about the subject:

____

Set **Question** yourself. Here's one thing I would like to know:

____

Go **Read.** (Remember to read words in groups without hesitating.)
Recite. (Annotate. Take notes in the margins.)
Review. Here's one thing I learned:

____

I. LITERAL COMPREHENSION

Reporter's Questions

Who? ______________________________

What? ______________________________

Why? ______________________________

When? ______________________________

Where? ______________________________

Topic ______________________________

Main Idea ______________________________

Three Details

1. ______________________________
2. ______________________________
3. ______________________________

New Words (Plus definitions)

1. ____________________

2. ____________________

3. ____________________

4. ____________________

One more word! ____________________

How I found it (context, word parts, dictionary) ____________________

How I use it ____________________

II. CRITICAL COMPREHENSION

List two opinions (use quotes!)

1. ____________________

2. ____________________

The viewpoint of the article is ____________________

III. AFFECTIVE COMPREHENSION

After reading this article, I believe ____________________

____

____

____

____

QUESTIONS????

Newsweek Worksheet

Understanding the News

Name ______________________________

Class ________________ Date ________________

Choose a news article from the current issue of *Newsweek.* (Look for the heading "Special Report," "International News," or "National Affairs." Then complete this worksheet).

Ready — **Survey** the material. Here's what I know about the subject:

____

Set — **Question** yourself. Here's one thing I would like to know:

____

Go — **Read.** (Remember to read words in groups without hesitating.)
Recite. (Annotate. Take notes in the margins.)
Review. Here's one thing I learned:

____

I. LITERAL COMPREHENSION

Reporter's Questions

Who? ____

What? ____

Why? ____

When? ____

Where? ____

Topic ____

Main Idea ____

Three Details

1. ____
2. ____
3. ____

New Words (Plus definitions)

1. ______________________________

2. ______________________________

3. ______________________________

4. ______________________________

One more word! ______________________________

How I found it (context, word parts, dictionary) ______________________________

How I use it ______________________________

II. CRITICAL COMPREHENSION

List two opinions (use quotes!)

1. ______________________________

2. ______________________________

The viewpoint of the article is ______________________________

III. AFFECTIVE COMPREHENSION

After reading this article, I believe ______________________________

____

____

____

____

QUESTIONS????

Newsweek Worksheet

Understanding the News

Name________________________________

Class ________________ **Date**________________

Choose a news article from the current issue of *Newsweek.* (Look for the heading "Special Report," "International News," or "National Affairs." Then complete this worksheet).

Ready **Survey** the material. Here's what I know about the subject:

____

Set **Question** yourself. Here's one thing I would like to know:

____

Go **Read.** (Remember to read words in groups without hesitating.)
Recite. (Annotate. Take notes in the margins.)
Review. Here's one thing I learned:

____

I. LITERAL COMPREHENSION

Reporter's Questions

Who? ____

What? ____

Why? ____

When? ____

Where? ____

Topic ____

Main Idea ____

Three Details

1. ____
2. ____
3. ____

New Words (Plus definitions)

1. ______________________________

2. ______________________________

3. ______________________________

4. ______________________________

One more word! ______________________________

How I found it (context, word parts, dictionary) ______________________________

How I use it ______________________________

II. CRITICAL COMPREHENSION

List two opinions (use quotes!)

1. ______________________________

2. ______________________________

The viewpoint of the article is ______________________________

III. AFFECTIVE COMPREHENSION

After reading this article, I believe ______________________________

____

____

____

____

QUESTIONS????

Newsweek Worksheet

Understanding the News

Name____________________________________

Class ________________ **Date**________________

Choose a news article from the current issue of *Newsweek.* (Look for the heading "Special Report," "International News," or "National Affairs." Then complete this worksheet).

Ready **Survey** the material. Here's what I know about the subject:

____

Set **Question** yourself. Here's one thing I would like to know:

____

Go **Read.** (Remember to read words in groups without hesitating.)
Recite. (Annotate. Take notes in the margins.)
Review. Here's one thing I learned:

____

I. LITERAL COMPREHENSION

Reporter's Questions

Who? ____

What? ____

Why? ____

When? ____

Where? ____

Topic ____

Main Idea ____

Three Details

1. ____
2. ____
3. ____

New Words (Plus definitions)

1. ______________________________

2. ______________________________

3. ______________________________

4. ______________________________

One more word! ______________________________

How I found it (context, word parts, dictionary) ______________________________

How I use it ______________________________

II. CRITICAL COMPREHENSION

List two opinions (use quotes!)

1. ______________________________

2. ______________________________

The viewpoint of the article is ______________________________

III. AFFECTIVE COMPREHENSION

After reading this article, I believe ______________________________

____

____

____

____

QUESTIONS????

Newsweek Worksheet

Understanding the News

Name ______________________

Class ______________ Date ______________

Choose a news article from the current issue of *Newsweek.* (Look for the heading "Special Report," "International News," or "National Affairs." Then complete this worksheet).

Ready **Survey** the material. Here's what I know about the subject:

____

Set **Question** yourself. Here's one thing I would like to know:

____

Go **Read.** (Remember to read words in groups without hesitating.)
Recite. (Annotate. Take notes in the margins.)
Review. Here's one thing I learned:

____

I. LITERAL COMPREHENSION

Reporter's Questions

Who? ______________________

What? ______________________

Why? ______________________

When? ______________________

Where? ______________________

Topic ______________________

Main Idea ______________________

Three Details

1. ______________________
2. ______________________
3. ______________________

New Words (Plus definitions)

1. ______________________________

2. ______________________________

3. ______________________________

4. ______________________________

One more word! ______________________________

How I found it (context, word parts, dictionary) ______________________________

How I use it ______________________________

II. CRITICAL COMPREHENSION

List two opinions (use quotes!)

1. ______________________________

2. ______________________________

The viewpoint of the article is ______________________________

III. AFFECTIVE COMPREHENSION

After reading this article, I believe ______________________________

____

____

____

____

QUESTIONS????

Newsweek Worksheet

Understanding the News

Name ______________________

Class ______________ **Date** ______________

Choose a news article from the current issue of *Newsweek.* (Look for the heading "Special Report," "International News," or "National Affairs." Then complete this worksheet).

Ready **Survey** the material. Here's what I know about the subject:

____

Set **Question** yourself. Here's one thing I would like to know:

____

Go **Read.** (Remember to read words in groups without hesitating.)
Recite. (Annotate. Take notes in the margins.)
Review. Here's one thing I learned:

____

I. LITERAL COMPREHENSION

Reporter's Questions

Who? ______________________

What? ______________________

Why? ______________________

When? ______________________

Where? ______________________

Topic ______________________

Main Idea ______________________

Three Details

1. ______________________
2. ______________________
3. ______________________

New Words (Plus definitions)

1. ______________________________

2. ______________________________

3. ______________________________

4. ______________________________

One more word! ______________________________

How I found it (context, word parts, dictionary) ______________________________

How I use it ______________________________

II. CRITICAL COMPREHENSION

List two opinions (use quotes!)

1. ______________________________

2. ______________________________

The viewpoint of the article is ______________________________

III. AFFECTIVE COMPREHENSION

After reading this article, I believe ______________________________

____

____

____

____

QUESTIONS????

Newsweek Worksheet

Understanding the News

Name ________________________________

Class ________________ **Date** ________________

Choose a news article from the current issue of *Newsweek.* (Look for the heading "Special Report," "International News," or "National Affairs." Then complete this worksheet).

Ready **Survey** the material. Here's what I know about the subject:

____

Set **Question** yourself. Here's one thing I would like to know:

____

Go **Read.** (Remember to read words in groups without hesitating.)
Recite. (Annotate. Take notes in the margins.)
Review. Here's one thing I learned:

____

I. LITERAL COMPREHENSION

Reporter's Questions

Who? ____

What? ____

Why? ____

When? ____

Where? ____

Topic ____

Main Idea ____

Three Details

1. ____
2. ____
3. ____

New Words (Plus definitions)

1. ______________________________

2. ______________________________

3. ______________________________

4. ______________________________

One more word! ______________________________

How I found it (context, word parts, dictionary) ______________________________

How I use it ______________________________

II. CRITICAL COMPREHENSION

List two opinions (use quotes!)

1. ______________________________

2. ______________________________

The viewpoint of the article is ______________________________

III. AFFECTIVE COMPREHENSION

After reading this article, I believe ______________________________

____

____

____

____

QUESTIONS????

UNIT 3

Understanding the Views

"Last Word" and "My Turn" Essays

Newsweek Worksheet

The Views

Name____________________________________

Class _________________ **Date**_________________

Choose a "The Last Word" or "My Turn" article. Practice SQ3R (see page 4) as you get ready to read and while you read. Then, answer the following questions:

I. LITERAL COMPREHENSION

Topic ____

Main Idea ____

Three Details

1. ____
2. ____
3. ____

New Words (Plus definitions)

1. ____
2. ____
3. ____
4. ____

One more word! ____________________________________

How I found it (context, word parts, dictionary) ____________________

How I use it ______________________________________

II. CRITICAL COMPREHENSION

The writer's *INTENT* (purpose) is: ____________________________

The writer's *ATTITUDE* (opinion) is: ___________________________

The writer's *TONE* (how opinion is expressed): _______________________

The *RHETORICAL MODE* is (argument, persuasion): _____________________

because ____

The writer's OPINION is ____

____

____

THREE ARGUMENTS that support this opinion are:

1. ____

2. ____

3. ____

One QUOTE that best expresses the opinion of the article is: ______________________

____

The writer's *CONCLUSION* is: ____

____

III. AFFECTIVE COMPREHENSION

Overall, the writer's argument was good/poor because: ______________________

____

I agree/disagree with the author because: ______________________________

____

____

____

____

QUESTIONS????

Newsweek Worksheet

The Views

Name______________________________________

Class __________________ **Date**__________________

Choose a "The Last Word" or "My Turn" article. Practice SQ3R (see page 4) as you get ready to read and while you read. Then, answer the following questions:

I. LITERAL COMPREHENSION

Topic ____

Main Idea ____

Three Details

1. ____
2. ____
3. ____

New Words (Plus definitions)

1. ____
2. ____
3. ____
4. ____

One more word! ______________________________________

How I found it (context, word parts, dictionary) ____________________

How I use it ____

II. CRITICAL COMPREHENSION

The writer's *INTENT* (purpose) is: _______________________________

The writer's *ATTITUDE* (opinion) is: ______________________________

The writer's *TONE* (how opinion is expressed): ________________________

The *RHETORICAL MODE* is (argument, persuasion): _____________________

because ____

The writer's OPINION is ______________________________

____

____

THREE ARGUMENTS that support this opinion are:

1. ______________________________

2. ______________________________

3. ______________________________

One QUOTE that best expresses the opinion of the article is: ______________________________

____

The writer's *CONCLUSION* is: ______________________________

____

III. AFFECTIVE COMPREHENSION

Overall, the writer's argument was good/poor because: ______________________________

____

I agree/disagree with the author because: ______________________________

____

____

____

____

QUESTIONS????

Newsweek Worksheet

The Views

Name ______________________________

Class ________________ **Date** ________________

Choose a "The Last Word" or "My Turn" article. Practice SQ3R (see page 4) as you get ready to read and while you read. Then, answer the following questions:

I. LITERAL COMPREHENSION

Topic ______________________________

Main Idea ______________________________

Three Details

1. ______________________________

2. ______________________________

3. ______________________________

New Words (Plus definitions)

1. ______________________________

2. ______________________________

3. ______________________________

4. ______________________________

One more word! ______________________________

How I found it (context, word parts, dictionary) ______________________________

How I use it ______________________________

II. CRITICAL COMPREHENSION

The writer's *INTENT* (purpose) is: ______________________________

The writer's *ATTITUDE* (opinion) is: ______________________________

The writer's *TONE* (how opinion is expressed): ______________________________

The *RHETORICAL MODE* is (argument, persuasion): ______________________________

because ______________________________

The writer's OPINION is ______________________________

____

____

THREE ARGUMENTS that support this opinion are:

1. ______________________________

2. ______________________________

3. ______________________________

One QUOTE that best expresses the opinion of the article is: ______________________________

____

The writer's *CONCLUSION* is: ______________________________

____

III. AFFECTIVE COMPREHENSION

Overall, the writer's argument was good/poor because: ______________________________

____

I agree/disagree with the author because: ______________________________

____

____

____

____

QUESTIONS????

Newsweek Worksheet

The Views

Name____

Class __________________ **Date**__________________

Choose a "The Last Word" or "My Turn" article. Practice SQ3R (see page 4) as you get ready to read and while you read. Then, answer the following questions:

I. LITERAL COMPREHENSION

Topic ____

Main Idea ____

Three Details

1. ____
2. ____
3. ____

New Words (Plus definitions)

1. ____
2. ____
3. ____
4. ____

One more word! ____

How I found it (context, word parts, dictionary) ______________________________

How I use it ____

II. CRITICAL COMPREHENSION

The writer's *INTENT* (purpose) is: ____

The writer's *ATTITUDE* (opinion) is: _______________________________________

The writer's *TONE* (how opinion is expressed): ________________________________

The *RHETORICAL MODE* is (argument, persuasion): ______________________________

because ____

The writer's OPINION is ____

____

____

THREE ARGUMENTS that support this opinion are:

1. ____

2. ____

3. ____

One QUOTE that best expresses the opinion of the article is: ____________________

____

The writer's *CONCLUSION* is: ____

____

III. AFFECTIVE COMPREHENSION

Overall, the writer's argument was good/poor because: ___________________________

____

I agree/disagree with the author because: ___________________________________

____

____

____

____

QUESTIONS????

Newsweek Worksheet

The Views

Name______________________________________

Class _________________ **Date**_________________

Choose a "The Last Word" or "My Turn" article. Practice SQ3R (see page 4) as you get ready to read and while you read. Then, answer the following questions:

I. LITERAL COMPREHENSION

Topic ____

Main Idea ______________________________________

Three Details

1. ______________________________________
2. ______________________________________
3. ______________________________________

New Words (Plus definitions)

1. ______________________________________
2. ______________________________________
3. ______________________________________
4. ______________________________________

One more word! ________________________________

How I found it (context, word parts, dictionary) ____________________

How I use it __________________________________

II. CRITICAL COMPREHENSION

The writer's *INTENT* (purpose) is: __________________________

The writer's *ATTITUDE* (opinion) is: _________________________

The writer's *TONE* (how opinion is expressed): ____________________

The *RHETORICAL MODE* is (argument, persuasion): __________________

because ____

The writer's OPINION is ______________________________

____

____

THREE ARGUMENTS that support this opinion are:

1. ______________________________

2. ______________________________

3. ______________________________

One QUOTE that best expresses the opinion of the article is: ______________________________

____

The writer's *CONCLUSION* is: ______________________________

____

III. AFFECTIVE COMPREHENSION

Overall, the writer's argument was good/poor because: ______________________________

____

I agree/disagree with the author because: ______________________________

____

____

____

____

QUESTIONS????

Newsweek Worksheet

The Views

Name ______________________________

Class ______________ **Date** ______________

Choose a "The Last Word" or "My Turn" article. Practice SQ3R (see page 4) as you get ready to read and while you read. Then, answer the following questions:

I. LITERAL COMPREHENSION

Topic ______________________________

Main Idea ______________________________

Three Details

1. ______________________________

2. ______________________________

3. ______________________________

New Words (Plus definitions)

1. ______________________________

2. ______________________________

3. ______________________________

4. ______________________________

One more word! ______________________________

How I found it (context, word parts, dictionary) ______________________________

How I use it ______________________________

II. CRITICAL COMPREHENSION

The writer's *INTENT* (purpose) is: ______________________________

The writer's *ATTITUDE* (opinion) is: ______________________________

The writer's *TONE* (how opinion is expressed): ______________________________

The *RHETORICAL MODE* is (argument, persuasion): ______________________________

because ______________________________

The writer's OPINION is ______________________________

____

____

THREE ARGUMENTS that support this opinion are:

1. ______________________________

2. ______________________________

3. ______________________________

One QUOTE that best expresses the opinion of the article is: ______________________________

____

The writer's *CONCLUSION* is: ______________________________

____

III. AFFECTIVE COMPREHENSION

Overall, the writer's argument was good/poor because: ______________________________

____

I agree/disagree with the author because: ______________________________

____

____

____

____

QUESTIONS????

Newsweek Worksheet

The Views

Name ______________________________

Class ______________ **Date** ______________

Choose a "The Last Word" or "My Turn" article. Practice SQ3R (see page 4) as you get ready to read and while you read. Then, answer the following questions:

I. LITERAL COMPREHENSION

Topic ______________________________

Main Idea ______________________________

Three Details

1. ______________________________
2. ______________________________
3. ______________________________

New Words (Plus definitions)

1. ______________________________
2. ______________________________
3. ______________________________
4. ______________________________

One more word! ______________________________

How I found it (context, word parts, dictionary) ______________________________

How I use it ______________________________

II. CRITICAL COMPREHENSION

The writer's *INTENT* (purpose) is: ______________________________

The writer's *ATTITUDE* (opinion) is: ______________________________

The writer's *TONE* (how opinion is expressed): ______________________________

The *RHETORICAL MODE* is (argument, persuasion): ______________________________

because ______________________________

The writer's OPINION is ______________________________

____

____

THREE ARGUMENTS that support this opinion are:

1. ______________________________

2. ______________________________

3. ______________________________

One QUOTE that best expresses the opinion of the article is: ______________________________

____

The writer's *CONCLUSION* is: ______________________________

____

III. AFFECTIVE COMPREHENSION

Overall, the writer's argument was good/poor because: ______________________________

____

I agree/disagree with the author because: ______________________________

____

____

____

____

QUESTIONS????

The Views

Name ______________________________

Class ________________ **Date** ________________

Choose a "The Last Word" or "My Turn" article. Practice SQ3R (see page 4) as you get ready to read and while you read. Then, answer the following questions:

I. LITERAL COMPREHENSION

Topic ______________________________

Main Idea ______________________________

Three Details

1. ______________________________

2. ______________________________

3. ______________________________

New Words (Plus definitions)

1. ______________________________

2. ______________________________

3. ______________________________

4. ______________________________

One more word! ______________________________

How I found it (context, word parts, dictionary) ______________________________

How I use it ______________________________

II. CRITICAL COMPREHENSION

The writer's *INTENT* (purpose) is: ______________________________

The writer's *ATTITUDE* (opinion) is: ______________________________

The writer's *TONE* (how opinion is expressed): ______________________________

The *RHETORICAL MODE* is (argument, persuasion): ______________________________

because ______________________________

The writer's OPINION is ____________________

____

____

THREE ARGUMENTS that support this opinion are:

1. ____________________
2. ____________________
3. ____________________

One QUOTE that best expresses the opinion of the article is: ____________________

____

The writer's *CONCLUSION* is: ____________________

____

III. AFFECTIVE COMPREHENSION

Overall, the writer's argument was good/poor because: ____________________

____

I agree/disagree with the author because: ____________________

____

____

____

____

QUESTIONS????

UNIT 4

Picture This

Analyzing Photos, Graphics, Cartoons, and Ads

The Photo Story

Name____

Class ____________________ **Date**____________________

Choose an article in the current issue of *Newsweek*. Review an accompanying photo, then answer the following questions.

I. LITERAL COMPREHENSION

Describe the photograph.

____

____

____

____

II. CRITICAL COMPREHENSION

What is implied, or suggested, by the photo?

____

____

____

____

III. AFFECTIVE COMPREHENSION

Explain why you believe the photo does or does not enhance the meaning of the article. What other types of photos would you add to help the reader?

____

____

____

____

____

____

____

Newsweek Worksheet

The Photo Story

Name______________________________

Class _______________ **Date**_______________

Choose an article in the current issue of *Newsweek*. Review an accompanying photo, then answer the following questions.

I. LITERAL COMPREHENSION

Describe the photograph.

____

____

____

____

II. CRITICAL COMPREHENSION

What is implied, or suggested, by the photo?

____

____

____

____

III. AFFECTIVE COMPREHENSION

Explain why you believe the photo does or does not enhance the meaning of the article. What other types of photos would you add to help the reader?

____

____

____

____

____

____

____

Newsweek Worksheet

The Photo Story

Name____

Class __________________ **Date**__________________

Choose an article in the current issue of *Newsweek*. Review an accompanying photo, then answer the following questions.

I. LITERAL COMPREHENSION

Describe the photograph.

____

____

____

____

II. CRITICAL COMPREHENSION

What is implied, or suggested, by the photo?

____

____

____

____

III. AFFECTIVE COMPREHENSION

Explain why you believe the photo does or does not enhance the meaning of the article. What other types of photos would you add to help the reader?

____

____

____

____

____

____

____

Newsweek Worksheet

The Photo Story

Name ______________________________

Class ______________ **Date** ______________

Choose an article in the current issue of *Newsweek*. Review an accompanying photo, then answer the following questions.

I. LITERAL COMPREHENSION

Describe the photograph.

II. CRITICAL COMPREHENSION

What is implied, or suggested, by the photo?

III. AFFECTIVE COMPREHENSION

Explain why you believe the photo does or does not enhance the meaning of the article. What other types of photos would you add to help the reader?

Newsweek Worksheet

The Photo Story

Name____________________________________

Class __________________ **Date**__________________

Choose an article in the current issue of *Newsweek*. Review an accompanying photo, then answer the following questions.

I. LITERAL COMPREHENSION

Describe the photograph.

____

____

____

____

II. CRITICAL COMPREHENSION

What is implied, or suggested, by the photo?

____

____

____

____

III. AFFECTIVE COMPREHENSION

Explain why you believe the photo does or does not enhance the meaning of the article. What other types of photos would you add to help the reader?

____

____

____

____

____

____

____

Newsweek Worksheet
The Photo Story

Name ________________________________

Class ________________ **Date** ________________

Choose an article in the current issue of *Newsweek*. Review an accompanying photo, then answer the following questions.

I. LITERAL COMPREHENSION

Describe the photograph.

____

____

____

____

II. CRITICAL COMPREHENSION

What is implied, or suggested, by the photo?

____

____

____

____

III. AFFECTIVE COMPREHENSION

Explain why you believe the photo does or does not enhance the meaning of the article. What other types of photos would you add to help the reader?

____

____

____

____

____

____

____

The Photo Story

Name____

Class __________________ **Date**__________________

Choose an article in the current issue of *Newsweek*. Review an accompanying photo, then answer the following questions.

I. LITERAL COMPREHENSION

Describe the photograph.

____

____

____

____

II. CRITICAL COMPREHENSION

What is implied, or suggested, by the photo?

____

____

____

____

III. AFFECTIVE COMPREHENSION

Explain why you believe the photo does or does not enhance the meaning of the article. What other types of photos would you add to help the reader?

____

____

____

____

____

____

____

Newsweek Worksheet

The Photo Story

Name ______________________________

Class ______________ **Date** ______________

Choose an article in the current issue of *Newsweek*. Review an accompanying photo, then answer the following questions.

I. LITERAL COMPREHENSION

Describe the photograph.

____

____

____

____

II. CRITICAL COMPREHENSION

What is implied, or suggested, by the photo?

____

____

____

____

III. AFFECTIVE COMPREHENSION

Explain why you believe the photo does or does not enhance the meaning of the article. What other types of photos would you add to help the reader?

____

____

____

____

____

____

____

Newsweek Worksheet
The Cartoon Story

Name____

Class ____________________ **Date**____________________

Choose a cartoon from the current issue of *Newsweek* and complete this worksheet.

I. LITERAL COMPREHENSION

1. Describe what you see in the cartoon.

____

____

2. Who or what do the figures and objects represent?

____

____

II. CRITICAL COMPREHENSION

What conclusions can be drawn from the cartoon?

____

____

____

____

____

III. AFFECTIVE COMPREHENSION

What is your opinion of this political cartoon? Is the cartoonist's statement a valid one? Explain why you agree or disagree.

____

____

____

____

____

Newsweek Worksheet

The Cartoon Story

Name ______________________________

Class ______________ **Date** ______________

Choose a cartoon from the current issue of *Newsweek* and complete this worksheet.

I. LITERAL COMPREHENSION

1. Describe what you see in the cartoon.

____

____

2. Who or what do the figures and objects represent?

____

____

II. CRITICAL COMPREHENSION

What conclusions can be drawn from the cartoon?

____

____

____

____

____

III. AFFECTIVE COMPREHENSION

What is your opinion of this political cartoon? Is the cartoonist's statement a valid one? Explain why you agree or disagree.

____

____

____

____

____

Newsweek Worksheet

The Cartoon Story

Name______________________________

Class ______________ **Date**______________

Choose a cartoon from the current issue of *Newsweek* and complete this worksheet.

I. LITERAL COMPREHENSION

1. Describe what you see in the cartoon.

____

____

2. Who or what do the figures and objects represent?

____

____

II. CRITICAL COMPREHENSION

What conclusions can be drawn from the cartoon?

____

____

____

____

____

III. AFFECTIVE COMPREHENSION

What is your opinion of this political cartoon? Is the cartoonist's statement a valid one? Explain why you agree or disagree.

____

____

____

____

____

Newsweek Worksheet

The Cartoon Story

Name ______________________________

Class ______________ **Date** ______________

Choose a cartoon from the current issue of *Newsweek* and complete this worksheet.

I. LITERAL COMPREHENSION

1. Describe what you see in the cartoon.

____

____

2. Who or what do the figures and objects represent?

____

____

II. CRITICAL COMPREHENSION

What conclusions can be drawn from the cartoon?

____

____

____

____

____

III. AFFECTIVE COMPREHENSION

What is your opinion of this political cartoon? Is the cartoonist's statement a valid one? Explain why you agree or disagree.

____

____

____

____

____

Newsweek Worksheet

The Cartoon Story

Name ______________________________

Class ______________ **Date** ______________

Choose a cartoon from the current issue of *Newsweek* and complete this worksheet.

I. LITERAL COMPREHENSION

1. Describe what you see in the cartoon.

____

____

2. Who or what do the figures and objects represent?

____

____

II. CRITICAL COMPREHENSION

What conclusions can be drawn from the cartoon?

____

____

____

____

____

III. AFFECTIVE COMPREHENSION

What is your opinion of this political cartoon? Is the cartoonist's statement a valid one? Explain why you agree or disagree.

____

____

____

____

____

Newsweek Worksheet

The Cartoon Story

Name ______________________________

Class ______________ **Date** ______________

Choose a cartoon from the current issue of *Newsweek* and complete this worksheet.

I. LITERAL COMPREHENSION

1. Describe what you see in the cartoon.

____

____

2. Who or what do the figures and objects represent?

____

____

II. CRITICAL COMPREHENSION

What conclusions can be drawn from the cartoon?

____

____

____

____

____

III. AFFECTIVE COMPREHENSION

What is your opinion of this political cartoon? Is the cartoonist's statement a valid one? Explain why you agree or disagree.

____

____

____

____

____

Newsweek Worksheet

The Cartoon Story

Name ______________________________

Class ________________ **Date** ________________

Choose a cartoon from the current issue of *Newsweek* and complete this worksheet.

I. LITERAL COMPREHENSION

1. Describe what you see in the cartoon.

____

____

2. Who or what do the figures and objects represent?

____

____

II. CRITICAL COMPREHENSION

What conclusions can be drawn from the cartoon?

____

____

____

____

____

III. AFFECTIVE COMPREHENSION

What is your opinion of this political cartoon? Is the cartoonist's statement a valid one? Explain why you agree or disagree.

____

____

____

____

____

Newsweek Worksheet

The Cartoon Story

Name____

Class __________________ **Date**__________________

Choose a cartoon from the current issue of *Newsweek* and complete this worksheet.

I. LITERAL COMPREHENSION

1. Describe what you see in the cartoon.

____

____

2. Who or what do the figures and objects represent?

____

____

II. CRITICAL COMPREHENSION

What conclusions can be drawn from the cartoon?

____

____

____

____

____

III. AFFECTIVE COMPREHENSION

What is your opinion of this political cartoon? Is the cartoonist's statement a valid one? Explain why you agree or disagree.

____

____

____

____

____

Newsweek Worksheet
The Graphics Story

Name____________________________________

Class ________________ **Date**________________

Charts, maps, and graphs often accompany articles and add to the reader's understanding of an issue.

Read an article in the current issue of *Newsweek*. Examine any accompanying graphics, then answer the questions below.

I. LITERAL COMPREHENSION

1. What is the main idea of the article or essay?

____

____

2. Explain the information in the chart or visual.

____

____

II. CRITICAL COMPREHENSION

1. What conclusions can be drawn from the chart or visual?

____

____

____

____

2. How does the visual help your understanding of the article or essay?

____

____

____

____

____

III. AFFECTIVE COMPREHENSION

Use the space below to create your own graphic based on the article or essay. Write a paragraph explaining its meaning.

Newsweek Worksheet

The Graphics Story

Name____

Class __________________ **Date**__________________

Charts, maps, and graphs often accompany articles and add to the reader's understanding of an issue.

Read an article in the current issue of *Newsweek.* Examine any accompanying graphics, then answer the questions below.

I. LITERAL COMPREHENSION

1. What is the main idea of the article or essay?

____

____

2. Explain the information in the chart or visual.

____

____

II. CRITICAL COMPREHENSION

1. What conclusions can be drawn from the chart or visual?

____

____

____

____

2. How does the visual help your understanding of the article or essay?

____

____

____

____

____

III. AFFECTIVE COMPREHENSION

Use the space below to create your own graphic based on the article or essay. Write a paragraph explaining its meaning.

The Graphics Story

Name____

Class __________________ **Date**__________________

Charts, maps, and graphs often accompany articles and add to the reader's understanding of an issue.

Read an article in the current issue of *Newsweek*. Examine any accompanying graphics, then answer the questions below.

I. LITERAL COMPREHENSION

1. What is the main idea of the article or essay?

____

____

2. Explain the information in the chart or visual.

____

____

II. CRITICAL COMPREHENSION

1. What conclusions can be drawn from the chart or visual?

____

____

____

____

2. How does the visual help your understanding of the article or essay?

____

____

____

____

____

III. AFFECTIVE COMPREHENSION

Use the space below to create your own graphic based on the article or essay. Write a paragraph explaining its meaning.

Newsweek Worksheet
The Graphics Story

Name______________________________________

Class __________________ **Date**__________________

Charts, maps, and graphs often accompany articles and add to the reader's understanding of an issue.

Read an article in the current issue of *Newsweek.* Examine any accompanying graphics, then answer the questions below.

I. LITERAL COMPREHENSION

1. What is the main idea of the article or essay?

____

____

2. Explain the information in the chart or visual.

____

____

II. CRITICAL COMPREHENSION

1. What conclusions can be drawn from the chart or visual?

____

____

____

____

2. How does the visual help your understanding of the article or essay?

____

____

____

____

____

III. AFFECTIVE COMPREHENSION

Use the space below to create your own graphic based on the article or essay. Write a paragraph explaining its meaning.

Newsweek Worksheet
The Graphics Story

Name____

Class _________________ **Date**_________________

Charts, maps, and graphs often accompany articles and add to the reader's understanding of an issue.

Read an article in the current issue of *Newsweek*. Examine any accompanying graphics, then answer the questions below.

I. LITERAL COMPREHENSION

1. What is the main idea of the article or essay?

____

____

2. Explain the information in the chart or visual.

____

____

II. CRITICAL COMPREHENSION

1. What conclusions can be drawn from the chart or visual?

____

____

____

____

2. How does the visual help your understanding of the article or essay?

____

____

____

____

____

III. AFFECTIVE COMPREHENSION

Use the space below to create your own graphic based on the article or essay. Write a paragraph explaining its meaning.

Newsweek Worksheet

The Graphics Story

Name ______________________________

Class ______________ **Date** ______________

Charts, maps, and graphs often accompany articles and add to the reader's understanding of an issue.

Read an article in the current issue of *Newsweek*. Examine any accompanying graphics, then answer the questions below.

I. LITERAL COMPREHENSION

1. What is the main idea of the article or essay?

____

____

2. Explain the information in the chart or visual.

____

____

II. CRITICAL COMPREHENSION

1. What conclusions can be drawn from the chart or visual?

____

____

____

____

2. How does the visual help your understanding of the article or essay?

____

____

____

____

____

III. AFFECTIVE COMPREHENSION

Use the space below to create your own graphic based on the article or essay. Write a paragraph explaining its meaning.

Newsweek Worksheet

The Graphics Story

Name ______________________________

Class ______________ **Date** ______________

Charts, maps, and graphs often accompany articles and add to the reader's understanding of an issue.

Read an article in the current issue of *Newsweek*. Examine any accompanying graphics, then answer the questions below.

I. LITERAL COMPREHENSION

1. What is the main idea of the article or essay?

____

____

2. Explain the information in the chart or visual.

____

____

II. CRITICAL COMPREHENSION

1. What conclusions can be drawn from the chart or visual?

____

____

____

____

2. How does the visual help your understanding of the article or essay?

____

____

____

____

____

III. AFFECTIVE COMPREHENSION

Use the space below to create your own graphic based on the article or essay. Write a paragraph explaining its meaning.

Newsweek Worksheet

The Graphics Story

Name ______________________________

Class ________________ **Date** ________________

Charts, maps, and graphs often accompany articles and add to the reader's understanding of an issue.

Read an article in the current issue of *Newsweek*. Examine any accompanying graphics, then answer the questions below.

I. LITERAL COMPREHENSION

1. What is the main idea of the article or essay?

____

____

2. Explain the information in the chart or visual.

____

____

II. CRITICAL COMPREHENSION

1. What conclusions can be drawn from the chart or visual?

____

____

____

____

2. How does the visual help your understanding of the article or essay?

____

____

____

____

____

III. AFFECTIVE COMPREHENSION

Use the space below to create your own graphic based on the article or essay. Write a paragraph explaining its meaning.

ANALYZING ADS

Advertisements are created to sell products or services.To get consumers to buy something or buy into an idea, advertisers often use clever propaganda techniques. ***Propaganda*** is a deliberate attempt to sway opinion. Here's a list of techniques advertisers use to create consumer interest:

Word Choice Particular words are chosen that relate to the product. These words are designed to stick in the reader's mind. These words may also produce an exaggerated image. Rhymes, alliteration, and superlatives are often used for this effect. For example, calling a candidate a *"star-spangled citizen"* is catchy and conveys a patriotic image.

Transfer A picture conveys an exaggerated impression. Often the product and picture are unrelated. For example, a beautiful model may be used in a perfume ad to suggest that whoever uses the perfume will look like the model.

Testimonial A famous person lends his or her name or photo to a product endorsement. The product or service being sold may be completely unrelated to the famous person's area of expertise. For example, a basketball player may be used to sell cereal. Because the famous person has a positive image, the consumer will relate it to the product.

Plain Folks The "average" person or family is used in an ad so that people can relate to the images. For example, a scene with a family sitting at a dinner table may be used to sell life insurance.

Card Stacking Statistical or other comparisons may create an exaggerated impression of the product. For example, stating that twice as many dentists surveyed use Brand X over any other brand may convince people to buy Brand X. However, the number of dentists surveyed may not be stated.

Bandwagon Stating that most people are using a product or service may convince the consumer that getting on the "bandwagon" is a good idea. For example, if the ad shows a large group of teenagers wearing a particular type of jeans, the reader may wish to "join the bunch."

Newsweek Worksheet

The Ad Story

Name ______________________________

Class ________________ **Date** ________________

Find an ad in the current issue of *Newsweek,* then answer the following questions based on your examination of the ad.

I. LITERAL COMPREHENSION

Describe the advertisement.

____

____

____

____

II. CRITICAL COMPREHENSION

Which propaganda technique is being used in this ad? Explain how it helps to sell the product or service.

____

____

____

____

III. AFFECTIVE COMPREHENSION

1. Explain why you believe the ad is or is not effective.

____

____

____

____

____

____

____

2. Using a different propaganda technique, write your own advertisement for the same product or service. Use the space below to create an image to accompany the ad, if you'd like.

Newsweek Worksheet

The Ad Story

Name ______________________________

Class ________________ **Date** ________________

Find an ad in the current issue of *Newsweek,* then answer the following questions based on your examination of the ad.

I. LITERAL COMPREHENSION

Describe the advertisement.

____

____

____

____

II. CRITICAL COMPREHENSION

Which propaganda technique is being used in this ad? Explain how it helps to sell the product or service.

____

____

____

____

III. AFFECTIVE COMPREHENSION

1. Explain why you believe the ad is or is not effective.

____

____

____

____

____

____

____

2. Using a different propaganda technique, write your own advertisement for the same product or service. Use the space below to create an image to accompany the ad, if you'd like.

Newsweek Worksheet

The Ad Story

Name______________________________

Class ________________ **Date**________________

Find an ad in the current issue of *Newsweek,* then answer the following questions based on your examination of the ad.

I. LITERAL COMPREHENSION

Describe the advertisement.

II. CRITICAL COMPREHENSION

Which propaganda technique is being used in this ad? Explain how it helps to sell the product or service.

III. AFFECTIVE COMPREHENSION

1. Explain why you believe the ad is or is not effective.

2. Using a different propaganda technique, write your own advertisement for the same product or service. Use the space below to create an image to accompany the ad, if you'd like.

The Ad Story

Name________________________________

Class ________________ **Date**________________

Find an ad in the current issue of *Newsweek,* then answer the following questions based on your examination of the ad.

I. LITERAL COMPREHENSION

Describe the advertisement.

II. CRITICAL COMPREHENSION

Which propaganda technique is being used in this ad? Explain how it helps to sell the product or service.

III. AFFECTIVE COMPREHENSION

1. Explain why you believe the ad is or is not effective.

2. Using a different propaganda technique, write your own advertisement for the same product or service. Use the space below to create an image to accompany the ad, if you'd like.

Newsweek Worksheet

The Ad Story

Name____

Class __________________ **Date**__________________

Find an ad in the current issue of *Newsweek,* then answer the following questions based on your examination of the ad.

I. LITERAL COMPREHENSION

Describe the advertisement.

____

____

____

____

II. CRITICAL COMPREHENSION

Which propaganda technique is being used in this ad? Explain how it helps to sell the product or service.

____

____

____

____

III. AFFECTIVE COMPREHENSION

1. Explain why you believe the ad is or is not effective.

____

____

____

____

____

____

____

2. Using a different propaganda technique, write your own advertisement for the same product or service. Use the space below to create an image to accompany the ad, if you'd like.

Newsweek Worksheet

The Ad Story

Name____

Class __________________ **Date**__________________

Find an ad in the current issue of *Newsweek,* then answer the following questions based on your examination of the ad.

I. LITERAL COMPREHENSION

Describe the advertisement.

____

____

____

____

II. CRITICAL COMPREHENSION

Which propaganda technique is being used in this ad? Explain how it helps to sell the product or service.

____

____

____

____

III. AFFECTIVE COMPREHENSION

1. Explain why you believe the ad is or is not effective.

____

____

____

____

____

____

____

2. Using a different propaganda technique, write your own advertisement for the same product or service. Use the space below to create an image to accompany the ad, if you'd like.

Newsweek Worksheet

The Ad Story

Name______________________________

Class ______________ Date______________

Find an ad in the current issue of *Newsweek,* then answer the following questions based on your examination of the ad.

I. LITERAL COMPREHENSION

Describe the advertisement.

____

____

____

____

II. CRITICAL COMPREHENSION

Which propaganda technique is being used in this ad? Explain how it helps to sell the product or service.

____

____

____

____

III. AFFECTIVE COMPREHENSION

1. Explain why you believe the ad is or is not effective.

____

____

____

____

____

____

____

2. Using a different propaganda technique, write your own advertisement for the same product or service. Use the space below to create an image to accompany the ad, if you'd like.

Newsweek Worksheet

The Ad Story

Name________________________________

Class ________________ **Date**______________

Find an ad in the current issue of *Newsweek,* then answer the following questions based on your examination of the ad.

I. LITERAL COMPREHENSION

Describe the advertisement.

____

____

____

____

II. CRITICAL COMPREHENSION

Which propaganda technique is being used in this ad? Explain how it helps to sell the product or service.

____

____

____

____

III. AFFECTIVE COMPREHENSION

1. Explain why you believe the ad is or is not effective.

____

____

____

____

____

____

____

2. Using a different propaganda technique, write your own advertisement for the same product or service. Use the space below to create an image to accompany the ad, if you'd like.

Unit 5

Beyond the News

The Departments

Newsweek Worksheet

Reviewing the Reviews

Name ________________________

Class __________ **Date** __________

Choose a review from the current issue of *Newsweek.* Then complete the worksheet.

I. LITERAL COMPREHENSION

1. What is being reviewed?

2. Describe the object of the review.

II. CRITICAL COMPREHENSION

1. What is the reviewer's opinion?

2. What arguments does the reviewer use to support the opinion?

III. AFFECTIVE COMPREHENSION

1. Explain why you are or are not convinced by the writer's argument.

2. Does the review spark your interest in what is being assessed? Why or why not?

Reviewing the Reviews

Name____

Class __________________ **Date**__________________

Choose a review from the current issue of *Newsweek.* Then complete the worksheet.

I. LITERAL COMPREHENSION

1. What is being reviewed?

____

____

2. Describe the object of the review.

____

____

____

____

____

II. CRITICAL COMPREHENSION

1. What is the reviewer's opinion?

____

____

____

____

2. What arguments does the reviewer use to support the opinion?

____

____

____

____

____

III. AFFECTIVE COMPREHENSION

1. Explain why you are or are not convinced by the writer's argument.

2. Does the review spark your interest in what is being assessed? Why or why not?

Newsweek Worksheet

Reviewing the Reviews

Name________________________________

Class ________________ **Date**________________

Choose a review from the current issue of *Newsweek.* Then complete the worksheet.

I. LITERAL COMPREHENSION

1. What is being reviewed?

2. Describe the object of the review.

II. CRITICAL COMPREHENSION

1. What is the reviewer's opinion?

2. What arguments does the reviewer use to support the opinion?

III. AFFECTIVE COMPREHENSION

1. Explain why you are or are not convinced by the writer's argument.

2. Does the review spark your interest in what is being assessed? Why or why not?

Newsweek Worksheet

Reviewing the Reviews

Name ______________________________

Class ________________ **Date** ________________

Choose a review from the current issue of *Newsweek.* Then complete the worksheet.

I. LITERAL COMPREHENSION

1. What is being reviewed?

____

____

2. Describe the object of the review.

____

____

____

____

____

II. CRITICAL COMPREHENSION

1. What is the reviewer's opinion?

____

____

____

____

2. What arguments does the reviewer use to support the opinion?

____

____

____

____

____

III. AFFECTIVE COMPREHENSION

1. Explain why you are or are not convinced by the writer's argument.

2. Does the review spark your interest in what is being assessed? Why or why not?

Newsweek Worksheet

Reviewing the Reviews

Name ______________________

Class ____________ **Date** ____________

Choose a review from the current issue of *Newsweek.* Then complete the worksheet.

I. LITERAL COMPREHENSION

1. What is being reviewed?

____

____

2. Describe the object of the review.

____

____

____

____

____

II. CRITICAL COMPREHENSION

1. What is the reviewer's opinion?

____

____

____

____

2. What arguments does the reviewer use to support the opinion?

____

____

____

____

____

III. AFFECTIVE COMPREHENSION

1. Explain why you are or are not convinced by the writer's argument.

2. Does the review spark your interest in what is being assessed? Why or why not?

Newsweek Worksheet

Reviewing the Reviews

Name____________________________________

Class __________________ **Date**__________________

Choose a review from the current issue of *Newsweek.* Then complete the worksheet.

I. LITERAL COMPREHENSION

1. What is being reviewed?

____

____

2. Describe the object of the review.

____

____

____

____

____

II. CRITICAL COMPREHENSION

1. What is the reviewer's opinion?

____

____

____

____

2. What arguments does the reviewer use to support the opinion?

____

____

____

____

____

III. AFFECTIVE COMPREHENSION

1. Explain why you are or are not convinced by the writer's argument.

2. Does the review spark your interest in what is being assessed? Why or why not?

Newsweek Worksheet

Reviewing the Reviews

Name____

Class __________________ **Date**__________________

Choose a review from the current issue of *Newsweek.* Then complete the worksheet.

I. LITERAL COMPREHENSION

1. What is being reviewed?

____

____

2. Describe the object of the review.

____

____

____

____

____

II. CRITICAL COMPREHENSION

1. What is the reviewer's opinion?

____

____

____

____

2. What arguments does the reviewer use to support the opinion?

____

____

____

____

____

III. AFFECTIVE COMPREHENSION

1. Explain why you are or are not convinced by the writer's argument.

2. Does the review spark your interest in what is being assessed? Why or why not?

Newsweek Worksheet

Reviewing the Reviews

Name ______________________________

Class ______________ **Date** ______________

Choose a review from the current issue of *Newsweek.* Then complete the worksheet.

I. LITERAL COMPREHENSION

1. What is being reviewed?

____

____

2. Describe the object of the review.

____

____

____

____

____

II. CRITICAL COMPREHENSION

1. What is the reviewer's opinion?

____

____

____

____

2. What arguments does the reviewer use to support the opinion?

____

____

____

____

____

III. AFFECTIVE COMPREHENSION

1. Explain why you are or are not convinced by the writer's argument.

2. Does the review spark your interest in what is being assessed? Why or why not?

Newsweek Worksheet

The Millenium Notebook—What's New for 2000?

Name ______________________________

Class ________________ **Date** ________________

Read the article in the "Millenium Notebook" feature in a current issue of *Newsweek,* then answer the following questions based on your reading.

I. LITERAL COMPREHENSION

1. What is the main idea of the article?

____

____

2. List three important details that support the main idea.

    1. ____

    2. ____

    3. ____

II. CRITICAL COMPREHENSION

1. Is the author's view an optimistic (positive) or a pessimistic (negative) one? Explain.

____

____

2. What conclusions about the year 2000 have you drawn as a result of this article?

____

____

____

3. How does the chart or sidebar help your understanding of the article?

____

____

III. AFFECTIVE COMPREHENSION

Create your own "Millennium Notebook" by researching an aspect of the coming century and writing an article about it.

Newsweek Worksheet

The Millenium Notebook—What's New for 2000?

Name ______________________________

Class ______________ **Date** ______________

Read the article in the "Millenium Notebook" feature in a current issue of *Newsweek,* then answer the following questions based on your reading.

I. LITERAL COMPREHENSION

1. What is the main idea of the article?

____

____

2. List three important details that support the main idea.

   1. ______________________________

   2. ______________________________

   3. ______________________________

II. CRITICAL COMPREHENSION

1. Is the author's view an optimistic (positive) or a pessimistic (negative) one? Explain.

____

____

2. What conclusions about the year 2000 have you drawn as a result of this article?

____

____

____

3. How does the chart or sidebar help your understanding of the article?

____

____

III. AFFECTIVE COMPREHENSION

Create your own "Millennium Notebook" by researching an aspect of the coming century and writing an article about it.

Newsweek Worksheet

The Millenium Notebook—What's New for 2000?

Name ______________________

Class ____________ **Date** ____________

Read the article in the "Millenium Notebook" feature in a current issue of *Newsweek*, then answer the following questions based on your reading.

I. LITERAL COMPREHENSION

1. What is the main idea of the article?

____

____

2. List three important details that support the main idea.

   1. ______________________
   2. ______________________
   3. ______________________

II. CRITICAL COMPREHENSION

1. Is the author's view an optimistic (positive) or a pessimistic (negative) one? Explain.

____

____

2. What conclusions about the year 2000 have you drawn as a result of this article?

____

____

____

3. How does the chart or sidebar help your understanding of the article?

____

____

III. AFFECTIVE COMPREHENSION

Create your own "Millennium Notebook" by researching an aspect of the coming century and writing an article about it.

The Millenium Notebook—What's New for 2000?

Name ______________________________

Class ________________ **Date** ________________

Read the article in the "Millenium Notebook" feature in a current issue of *Newsweek,* then answer the following questions based on your reading.

I. LITERAL COMPREHENSION

1. What is the main idea of the article?

____

____

2. List three important details that support the main idea.

1. ______________________________
2. ______________________________
3. ______________________________

II. CRITICAL COMPREHENSION

1. Is the author's view an optimistic (positive) or a pessimistic (negative) one? Explain.

____

____

2. What conclusions about the year 2000 have you drawn as a result of this article?

____

____

____

3. How does the chart or sidebar help your understanding of the article?

____

____

III. AFFECTIVE COMPREHENSION

Create your own "Millennium Notebook" by researching an aspect of the coming century and writing an article about it.

Newsweek Worksheet

Focus on Cyberscope

Name______________________________________

Class __________________ **Date**__________________

Newsweek's Cyberscope feature focuses on innovations in computers and the Internet. Using a current issue of *Newsweek*, choose two of the selections that interest you, then write a short summary of each one. Then, do some research on your own to create your own Cyberscope selection.

1. Topic: ______________________________________

Summary: ____

2. Topic: ______________________________________

Summary: ____

Here's my "Cyberscope Bit":

Topic: ______________________________________

Newsweek Worksheet

Focus on Cyberscope

Name______________________________________

Class __________________ **Date**__________________

Newsweek's Cyberscope feature focuses on innovations in computers and the Internet. Using a current issue of *Newsweek*, choose two of the selections that interest you, then write a short summary of each one. Then, do some research on your own to create your own Cyberscope selection.

1. Topic: ____

Summary: ____

2. Topic: ____

Summary: ____

Here's my "Cyberscope Bit":

Topic: ____

Newsweek Worksheet

Focus on Cyberscope

Name______________________________________

Class __________________ **Date**__________________

Newsweek's Cyberscope feature focuses on innovations in computers and the Internet. Using a current issue of *Newsweek*, choose two of the selections that interest you, then write a short summary of each one. Then, do some research on your own to create your own Cyberscope selection.

1. Topic: ______________________________________

Summary: ______________________________________

2. Topic: ______________________________________

Summary: ______________________________________

Here's my "Cyberscope Bit":

Topic: ______________________________________

Newsweek Worksheet

Focus on Cyberscope

Name______________________________

Class ______________ **Date**______________

Newsweek's Cyberscope feature focuses on innovations in computers and the Internet. Using a current issue of *Newsweek*, choose two of the selections that interest you, then write a short summary of each one. Then, do some research on your own to create your own Cyberscope selection.

1. Topic: ______________________________

Summary: ______________________________

2. Topic: ______________________________

Summary: ______________________________

Here's my "Cyberscope Bit":

Topic: ______________________________

Newsweek Worksheet

Focus on Periscope

Name ______________________________

Class ______________ **Date** ______________

Newsweek's Periscope feature focuses on interesting issues in political and cultural events. The format may be a short "blurb," a chart, map, or some other eye-catching graphic (check out the "Conventional Wisdom Watch"!). Using a current issue of *Newsweek,* choose two of the selections that interest you, then write a short summary of each one. Then, do some research on your own to create your own Periscope selection.

1. Topic: ______________________________

Summary: ______________________________

____

____

____

____

2. Topic: ______________________________

Summary: ______________________________

____

____

____

____

Here's my "Periscope Bit":
(Write a paragraph or create a Conventional Wisdom Watch or other graphic.)

Topic: ______________________________

Newsweek Worksheet

Focus on Periscope

Name ______________________________

Class ________________ **Date** ________________

Newsweek's Periscope feature focuses on interesting issues in political and cultural events. The format may be a short "blurb," a chart, map, or some other eye-catching graphic (check out the "Conventional Wisdom Watch"!). Using a current issue of *Newsweek*, choose two of the selections that interest you, then write a short summary of each one. Then, do some research on your own to create your own Periscope selection.

1. Topic: ______________________________

Summary: ______________________________

____

____

____

____

2. Topic: ______________________________

Summary: ______________________________

____

____

____

____

Here's my "Periscope Bit":
(Write a paragraph or create a Conventional Wisdom Watch or other graphic.)

Topic: ______________________________

Newsweek Worksheet

Focus on Periscope

Name____

Class ____________________ **Date**____________________

Newsweek's Periscope feature focuses on interesting issues in political and cultural events. The format may be a short "blurb," a chart, map, or some other eye-catching graphic (check out the "Conventional Wisdom Watch"!). Using a current issue of *Newsweek,* choose two of the selections that interest you, then write a short summary of each one. Then, do some research on your own to create your own Periscope selection.

1. Topic: ____

Summary: ____

2. Topic: ____

Summary: ____

Here's my "Periscope Bit":
(Write a paragraph or create a Conventional Wisdom Watch or other graphic.)

Topic: ____

Newsweek Worksheet

Focus on Periscope

Name ______________________

Class ____________ **Date** ____________

Newsweek's Periscope feature focuses on interesting issues in political and cultural events. The format may be a short "blurb," a chart, map, or some other eye-catching graphic (check out the "Conventional Wisdom Watch"!). Using a current issue of *Newsweek*, choose two of the selections that interest you, then write a short summary of each one. Then, do some research on your own to create your own Periscope selection.

1. Topic: ______________________

Summary: ______________________

____

____

____

____

2. Topic: ______________________

Summary: ______________________

____

____

____

____

Here's my "Periscope Bit":
(Write a paragraph or create a Conventional Wisdom Watch or other graphic.)

Topic: ______________________

Newsweek Worksheet
Focus on Newsmakers

Name ____________________

Class ____________ Date ____________

Newsweek's Newsmakers feature focuses on people in the news. Using a current issue of *Newsweek*, choose two of the selections that interest you, then write a short summary of each one. Then, do some research on your own (you might like to add a photo from a magazine) to create your own "Newsmakers Bit."

1. Topic: ____________________

Summary: ____________________

____

____

____

____

2. Topic: ____________________

Summary: ____________________

____

____

____

____

Here's my "Newsmakers Bit":

Topic: ____________________

____

____

____

____

____

____

Newsweek Worksheet

Focus on Newsmakers

Name____________________________________

Class ________________ **Date**________________

Newsweek's Newsmakers feature focuses on people in the news. Using a current issue of *Newsweek*, choose two of the selections that interest you, then write a short summary of each one. Then, do some research on your own (you might like to add a photo from a magazine) to create your own "Newsmakers Bit."

1. Topic: ____________________________________

Summary: ____________________________________

2. Topic: ____________________________________

Summary: ____________________________________

Here's my "Newsmakers Bit":

Topic: ____________________________________

Newsweek Worksheet

Focus on Newsmakers

Name ______________________________

Class ______________ **Date** ______________

Newsweek's Newsmakers feature focuses on people in the news. Using a current issue of *Newsweek*, choose two of the selections that interest you, then write a short summary of each one. Then, do some research on your own (you might like to add a photo from a magazine) to create your own "Newsmakers Bit."

1. Topic: ______________________________

Summary: ______________________________

____

____

____

____

2. Topic: ______________________________

Summary: ______________________________

____

____

____

____

Here's my "Newsmakers Bit":

Topic: ______________________________

____

____

____

____

____

Newsweek Worksheet

Focus on Newsmakers

Name____

Class __________________ **Date**__________________

Newsweek's Newsmakers feature focuses on people in the news. Using a current issue of *Newsweek,* choose two of the selections that interest you, then write a short summary of each one. Then, do some research on your own (you might like to add a photo from a magazine) to create your own "Newsmakers Bit."

1. Topic: ____

Summary: ____

2. Topic: ____

Summary: ____

Here's my "Newsmakers Bit":

Topic: ____

Newsweek Worksheet

Focus on Perspectives

Name ______________________________

Class ______________ Date ______________

Newsweek's Perspectives feature focuses on political cartoons and short quotes taken from current figures in the news. Choose five quotes from a current issue of *Newsweek*, write the name of the speaker, and explain the quote's relevance.

QUOTE #1

Speaker: ______________________________

Meaning: ______________________________

____

____

QUOTE #2

Speaker: ______________________________

Meaning: ______________________________

____

____

QUOTE #3

Speaker: ______________________________

Meaning: ______________________________

____

____

QUOTE #4

Speaker: ______________________________

Meaning: ______________________________

____

____

QUOTE #5

Speaker: ______________________________

Meaning: ____

____

____

Newsweek Worksheet

Focus on Perspectives

Name ____________________

Class ____________ **Date** ____________

Newsweek's Perspectives feature focuses on political cartoons and short quotes taken from current figures in the news. Choose five quotes from a current issue of *Newsweek*, write the name of the speaker, and explain the quote's relevance.

QUOTE #1

Speaker: ____________________

Meaning: ____________________

____

____

QUOTE #2

Speaker: ____________________

Meaning: ____________________

____

____

QUOTE #3

Speaker: ____________________

Meaning: ____________________

____

____

QUOTE #4

Speaker: ____________________

Meaning: ____________________

____

____

QUOTE #5

Speaker: ______________________________________

Meaning: ____

____

____

Newsweek Worksheet
Focus on Perspectives

Name____

Class __________________ **Date**__________________

Newsweek's Perspectives feature focuses on political cartoons and short quotes taken from current figures in the news. Choose five quotes from a current issue of *Newsweek,* write the name of the speaker, and explain the quote's relevance.

QUOTE #1

Speaker: ____

Meaning: ____

QUOTE #2

Speaker: ____

Meaning: ____

QUOTE #3

Speaker: ____

Meaning: ____

QUOTE #4

Speaker: ____

Meaning: ____

QUOTE #5

Speaker: ______________________________

Meaning: ______________________________

____

____

Newsweek Worksheet

Focus on Perspectives

Name____________________________________

Class ________________ **Date**________________

Newsweek's Perspectives feature focuses on political cartoons and short quotes taken from current figures in the news. Choose five quotes from a current issue of *Newsweek*, write the name of the speaker, and explain the quote's relevance.

QUOTE #1

Speaker: ____________________________________

Meaning: ____

QUOTE #2

Speaker: ____________________________________

Meaning: ____

QUOTE #3

Speaker: ____________________________________

Meaning: ____

QUOTE #4

Speaker: ____________________________________

Meaning: ____

QUOTE #5

Speaker: ______________________________

Meaning: ____

____

____

Newsweek Worksheet

Focus on Letters to the Editor

Name ______________________________

Class ________________ **Date** ________________

Newsweek's Letters to the Editor features focus on comments from readers concerning articles and essays that have appeared in recent issues. Choose three letters in a current issue of *Newsweek,* then answer the questions on the worksheet.

LETTER #1

1. Briefly explain the article being commented on.

____

____

____

2. What is the writer's opinion? Based on what you know, does the writer make a good point?

____

____

____

____

LETTER #2

1. Briefly explain the article being commented on.

____

____

____

2. What is the writer's opinion? Based on what you know, does the writer make a good point?

____

____

____

____

LETTER #3

1. Briefly explain the article being commented on.

2. What is the writer's opinion? Based on what you know, does the writer make a good point?

Newsweek Worksheet

Focus on Letters to the Editor

Name ______________________________

Class ______________ **Date** ______________

Newsweek's Letters to the Editor features focus on comments from readers concerning articles and essays that have appeared in recent issues. Choose three letters in a current issue of *Newsweek*, then answer the questions on the worksheet.

LETTER #1

1. Briefly explain the article being commented on.

____

____

____

2. What is the writer's opinion? Based on what you know, does the writer make a good point?

____

____

____

____

LETTER #2

1. Briefly explain the article being commented on.

____

____

____

2. What is the writer's opinion? Based on what you know, does the writer make a good point?

____

____

____

____

LETTER #3

1. Briefly explain the article being commented on.

2. What is the writer's opinion? Based on what you know, does the writer make a good point?

Newsweek Worksheet

Focus on Letters to the Editor

Name ____________________

Class ____________ **Date** ____________

Newsweek's Letters to the Editor features focus on comments from readers concerning articles and essays that have appeared in recent issues. Choose three letters in a current issue of *Newsweek,* then answer the questions on the worksheet.

LETTER #1

1. Briefly explain the article being commented on.

2. What is the writer's opinion? Based on what you know, does the writer make a good point?

LETTER #2

1. Briefly explain the article being commented on.

2. What is the writer's opinion? Based on what you know, does the writer make a good point?

LETTER #3

1. Briefly explain the article being commented on.

2. What is the writer's opinion? Based on what you know, does the writer make a good point?

Newsweek Worksheet

Focus on Letters to the Editor

Name ______________________________

Class ______________ Date ______________

Newsweek's Letters to the Editor features focus on comments from readers concerning articles and essays that have appeared in recent issues. Choose three letters in a current issue of *Newsweek,* then answer the questions on the worksheet.

LETTER #1

1. Briefly explain the article being commented on.

____

____

____

2. What is the writer's opinion? Based on what you know, does the writer make a good point?

____

____

____

____

LETTER #2

1. Briefly explain the article being commented on.

____

____

____

2. What is the writer's opinion? Based on what you know, does the writer make a good point?

____

____

____

____

LETTER #3

1. Briefly explain the article being commented on.

2. What is the writer's opinion? Based on what you know, does the writer make a good point?

Newsweek Worksheet

Focus on Letters

Name______________________________

Class _______________ **Date**_______________

NOW . . . write your own letter to the Editors of *Newsweek*, responding to a featured article in a current issue.

Newsweek Worksheet

Focus on Letters

Name____

Class __________________ **Date**__________________

NOW . . . write your own letter to the Editors of *Newsweek,* responding to a featured article in a current issue.

Newsweek Worksheet

Focus on Letters

Name______________________________________

Class __________________ **Date**__________________

NOW . . . write your own letter to the Editors of *Newsweek,* responding to a featured article in a current issue.

Newsweek Worksheet

Focus on Letters

Name ______________________________

Class ______________ **Date** ______________

NOW . . . write your own letter to the Editors of *Newsweek*, responding to a featured article in a current issue.

UNIT 6

Talk About It, Write About It

Writing and Collaborative Activities

Unit 2: Understanding the News

1. Working with a group, create a list of questions to test your understanding of any of the articles in this unit. Write the answers to the questions in an outline, map, or summary. Make sure the summary has a clear thesis statement, along with an introduction, body, and a conclusion. Revise for spelling and grammar.
2. List all the quotes in the article on one side of a page, then write your response on the other side.
3. With your group, brainstorm (throw out ideas), freewrite (non-stop writing for a few minutes), or list possible articles for a local news item. Then research the item (anything pertinent to your community— for example, education, crime), and interview people using the journalist's Five W's (see page 2). Write your own article.
4. Be creative! Invent your own "newsworthy" topic, then present it as an article. Choose a specific rhetorical mode (see page 4), and read and compare essays within your group.

Unit 3: Understanding the Views

1. Using a "My Turn" or "The Last Word" article, make a list of all the arguments presented in the essay. Then, respond to each one of the articles on paper.
2. Choose a "My Turn" or "The Last Word" article, and prepare notes for a formal debate on the issue that you will perform with your group. For example, three people can take the side of the writer, and three others can take the opposing side.
3. Respond to a "My Turn" essay with your own essay. This project may also be done in a group, with several people working on the same response.
4. Do you have strong feelings about an issue? Write your own "My Turn" essay. You might even try submitting it to the editors of *Newsweek.*

Unit 4: Picture This

1. Choose any photograph in your issue of *Newsweek,* then write a summary explaining its meaning and relevance to the article.
2. Find a photograph (from a magazine, newspaper, or personal album), and create your own story about it. Compare projects with your group.
3. In your group, find a *Newsweek* article and create a graphic (chart, graph, etc.) that helps explain it.
4. Find an ad in *Newsweek* and identify the propaganda technique used. Create your own ad for the same product. Share the results with your group. See if they can identify the technique you employed.
5. Choose any product or service that you and your group can write ads about. Share them with one another. Create your own product or service, then formulate an ad and share it with your group.

Unit 5: Beyond the News

1. Read a current review in *Newsweek*, then write a response to it. The members of your group may all write about the same review or choose to write reviews about different subjects.
2. Write your own review of a book, movie, play, restaurant, or special event. Share it with your group.
3. Research and write an article for the Millennium Notebook. Choose any topic that will be of relevance in the coming century.
4. Have fun creating your own page of news in either the Cyberscope, Periscope, Newsmakers, or Perspective format. Each member of the group may create a different page. Pages may be based on current events in society at large, or even your own classroom.
5. Write a letter to *Newsweek* responding to any issue in a current edition. You may work alone or with your group.
6. Create your own mini-*Newsweek* magazine. Each member of the group may edit a different portion of the "magazine." Don't forget to include creative artwork and photos. Who knows? You may be headed for a career on the *Newsweek* staff!